C000011035

HOPE

Bright Ideas for Happier Days

lucy lane

summersdale

An Hachette UK Company
www.hachette.co.uk

Summersdale Publishers Ltd
Part of Octopus Publishing Group Limited
Carmelite House
50 Victoria Embankment
LONDON
EC4Y 0DZ
UK

www.summersdale.com

Printed and bound in the Czech Republic

ISBN: 978-1-80007-206-0

Substantial discounts on bulk quantities of Summersdale books are available to corporations, professional associations and other organisations. For details contact general enquiries: telephone: +44 (0) 1243 771107 or email: enquiries@summersdale.com.

INTRODUCTION

We could all use a little more hope, couldn't we? When the media is filled overwhelmingly with bad news, it can feel like there's no chance of things getting better or that there's nothing to look forward to. But hope – that little voice saying that something good will happen – is a powerful force that will give you the strength to carry on when everything seems to be against you. This book is filled with tips and inspiration to help you cultivate hope, positivity and resilience in yourself, spread a little bit of goodness to those around you and develop a more optimistic outlook on life. After all, there is so much in this world to be hopeful for.

Hope is being able
to see that there is
light despite all of
the darkness.

Desmond Tutu

ROLL WITH IT

In order to stay hopeful, it's important to be flexible about the journey to reaching your goals. During life-changing events or times of upheaval, it's easy to feel like a failure for not achieving your ambitions or not making as much progress as you think you should. But just consider for a moment about how mad it is to expect yourself to carry on at the same rate when the world and your life have changed so much. Go easy on yourself, and remember that, just as life has twists and turns, so will the paths to your goals – and sometimes you may need to adapt your goals accordingly. Viewing these changes as a natural part of your journey will help you maintain your hope and motivation.

IF EVERYTHING
WAS PERFECT,
YOU WOULD
NEVER LEARN
AND YOU
WOULD NEVER
GROW.

Beyoncé

That is one good thing
about this world...
there are always sure
to be more springs.

L. M. Montgomery

KEEP LOOKING FORWARD

If you are getting bogged down in the monotony of everyday life, remember to make plans to do things that make you happy. Your plan might be something really small, like a takeaway and film night or a woodland walk, or something bigger like a holiday, but the important thing is that you've got something in your diary to look forward to. This will help you maintain hope and positivity for the future, and motivate you to keep going through hard times.

Turn your face
toward the sun and
the shadows will
fall behind you.

Māori proverb

POSITIVE PALS

Who is the most positive person you know? Maybe it's your mother, your best friend or one of your work colleagues. Call them up for a chat or arrange to meet for lunch – you'll be surprised how much of a difference it makes to your own outlook to hang out with someone so hopeful and positive. Surround yourself with love and optimism and it'll soon rub off on you.

Together we can ensure that **tomorrow** will be a good day.

Captain Sir Tom Moore

PRACTISE GRATITUDE

When it seems like there is nothing to be hopeful about, it helps to remember all the good things in your life. Try listing five things you're grateful for: they could be big things, like your family or home, or little things like your morning coffee or a new episode of your favourite show. You'll probably think of way more than five! Focusing on the positives in your life will encourage you to be hopeful for good things in your future.

I don't think
of all the misery,
but of the beauty
that still remains.

Anne Frank

SPREAD THE LOVE

It's always lovely to do nice things for other people, but when you're feeling low and hopeless that might seem like too much to ask. How can you spread hope and cheer when you don't have any yourself? In this situation, random acts of kindness might be just the thing to create hope not just for others but for yourself too. You could help an elderly person with their shopping bags, send some chocolates to your best friend, buy a coffee for the next person in line or compliment the first three people you speak to today. The positive vibes you create will brighten that person's day and fill you with optimism too. You might even inspire people to pay it forward and carry out their own acts of kindness. What instils a sense of hope more than sending just a little bit more goodness out into the world?

Hope is not something
that you have. Hope
is something that
you create, with
your actions.

Alexandria Ocasio-Cortez

We must **accept**
finite disappointment,
but never lose
infinite **hope**.

Martin Luther King Jr

THE GREAT OUTDOORS

There's nothing like a bit of fresh air to help lift your spirits. Spending time outside in nature is linked to improved mood, energy and confidence, and can help to alleviate anxiety. Find a green space near you and spend some time being mindful of your surroundings – nature's beauty and tranquillity are inspiring and can help you feel calmly optimistic and refreshed.

No matter how dark
the skies may be, the sun
is shining somewhere
and will eventually
come smiling through.

P. G. Wodehouse

BEST-CASE SCENARIO

Far too many of us focus on the worst possible outcome with new opportunities or events. When bad things have happened in the past, it's hard to remember that a negative outcome is not always guaranteed. If you catch yourself thinking the worst about a new situation, take a minute to consider what the best possible outcome (or any positive outcome) would be. Write it down if it helps. This will remind you that good things are always possible!

Don't ever make
decisions based on
fear. Make decisions
based on **hope**
and possibility.

Michelle Obama

LOVE LETTERS

These days, communication is easier than ever, but we still often feel disconnected from the people around us. Try sending letters or postcards to a friend, or find a pen-pal from further afield on a website like PenPal World or Global Penfriends. You'll both get those warm feelings of anticipation when waiting for a reply, and sending and receiving handwritten letters full of positivity will help restore your faith and hope in humanity.

Great things are
done by a series
of small things
brought together.

Vincent van Gogh

ONE STEP AT A TIME

When you're feeling overwhelmed by your goals and the things that prevent you from achieving them, remember: you don't have to do everything today! Pause, take a few deep breaths and focus only on the very next thing you have to do. This step is all you have to concern yourself with and, once you've taken it, you only need to focus on the step after that. One step at a time is all it takes to keep moving forward.

Real change, enduring
change, happens
one step at a time.

Ruth Bader Ginsburg

It does not **matter**
how **slowly** you
go as **long** as
you do not **stop**.

Confucius

You must not lose faith
in humanity… if a few
drops of the ocean are
dirty, the ocean does
not become dirty.

Mahatma Gandhi

IT'S NOT ALL DOOM AND GLOOM

These days, it seems like we're constantly bombarded with bad news in the press, on the internet and on social media. It's important to stay informed about what's going on, but too much bad news can cultivate anxiety and a "doom-and-gloom" attitude, making it hard to be hopeful. Limit your bad news intake by setting aside a short period each day to read or watch the news. It's a good idea to do this in the morning, as hearing negative news stories before bed might fill you with worry and make it hard to sleep. Once you're up-to-date, try to avoid scrolling through news apps and social media channels the rest of the day. Better still, stock up on good news stories from websites such as Positive News or Good News Network. You'll soon be reminded that there are plenty of things to be hopeful about.

I DO NOT BELIEVE THAT ANY DARKNESS WILL ENDURE.

J. R. R. Tolkien

It is the same with
people as it is with
riding a bike. Only
when moving can one
comfortably maintain
one's balance.

Albert Einstein

BE MINDFUL

It's easy to obsess over past events or worry about the future, but practising mindfulness will help you reconnect with the present moment. Mindfulness means focusing on the world around you, and it's linked to improved well-being and increased enjoyment in life. Spend five minutes focusing on what you can see, hear or feel, or concentrate on your breathing and the sensations of your body. Doing this every day might help you let go of pessimistic thoughts and find joy in the moment.

If you have good
thoughts it will
shine out of your **face**
like **sunbeams**
and you will always
look **lovely**.

Roald Dahl

HOPE GROWS

Because of their association with growth, new life and rejuvenation, plants are an excellent symbol of hope. For a quick dose of positivity, bring nature into your home with colourful flowers, or, if you'd prefer something more lasting, adopt a new house plant. Caring for your plant and seeing it grow will help you feel a calm sense of optimism for your own growth. Plus, house plants can improve your home's air quality, aiding your focus and mood. It's win-win!

There are always
flowers for those who
want to see them.

Henri Matisse

GET PERSPECTIVE

It's easy for negative thoughts to drown out hope and optimism, but you don't have to accept these thoughts at face value – instead, try to put them into perspective. Being hopeful isn't about being rosy and cheerful 100 per cent of the time, but about how you deal with challenges and the negative thoughts that arise from them. Maybe something in your life didn't go to plan; if so, remember that it's just one thing, and it doesn't mean that everything else will go wrong too. Instead of thinking "Nothing ever goes right for me" or "I'm not good at anything," try reframing these thoughts to "This one thing didn't quite work out," or "I'm not so good at this particular thing." This will help put the problem into perspective so that you're able to accept it and move forward. Reframing your thoughts like this will help you keep negative events separate from your own identity, and will make it much easier for you to be hopeful instead of pessimistic about future opportunities.

I **trust** that everything happens for a **reason**, even if we are not **wise** enough to see it.

Oprah Winfrey

There are two ways of spreading light: to be the candle, or the mirror that reflects it.

Edith Wharton

A WILLING VOLUNTEER

Sometimes, the best way to restore your hope in humanity is by helping others. Not only is volunteering an excellent way contribute to society and help those in need, but it helps to build a sense of purpose and pride in yourself too. Pick a cause or charity that's meaningful to you and get involved! You'll have the chance to make a positive impact, and you'll be surrounded by people who inspire hope by doing good.

If you go out and
make some **good**
things happen, you
will fill the **world**
with hope, you will fill
yourself with **hope**.

Barack Obama

EMBRACE YOUR JOURNEY

Try to find joy in the process of reaching your goals, not simply in the results. If you are only ever focused on the outcome, you'll be easily disappointed and frustrated if the result isn't what you wanted, or if things didn't go to plan. Say you spent ages working on a pitch for a work project you really cared about, but in the end you didn't get the go-ahead. It would be easy to think the whole endeavour was a huge waste of time. But you will have learned so much from the experience that you can apply to your work in future, and if you enjoyed the research then it was worthwhile! If you view your experiences in this way then you'll feel less downhearted if things don't turn out how you expected. You'll also be able to find positive meaning in the journey and maintain a more optimistic perspective on your life.

If you fell down
yesterday, stand
up today.

H. G. Wells

OPTIMISM IS THE FUEL DRIVING EVERY FIGHT I'VE BEEN IN.

Kamala Harris

GET YOUR BODY MOVING

Everyone knows that exercise is good for your physical health, but it also has many benefits for your mental health: it can reduce stress and worry, help you sleep better and improve your self-worth and outlook of positivity to no end. Exercise releases endorphins (your feel-good hormones), which boost not just your mood but your outlook, making you more positive and hopeful about the future. That's why getting your body moving is one of the best tools at your disposal for building resilience and coping with life's challenges in a healthy way. Remember that exercise doesn't have to be about losing weight or changing the way you look – regular activity is a way of investing in your mind and body for the present and the future, helping you to feel more powerful and confident about yourself and your abilities. You don't have to be a fitness nut – just a little bit of exercise is enough to reap the benefits, as long as it becomes a regular habit. So get those running shoes on!

Fear never **builds** the **future,** but hope does.

Joe Biden

Even if people think
I can't do it, I should
not lose hope.

Malala Yousafzai

DON'T LOOK BACK

Do you constantly find yourself dwelling on your past mistakes and fixating on what you could have done differently? This is a totally natural response, but it's not helpful. In fact, it makes things worse! Beating yourself up about things that have already happened just leads to a loss in confidence. You can't change the past and, besides, everyone makes mistakes. When you catch yourself obsessing over past incidents, acknowledge those thoughts, then remind yourself that tomorrow is a brand new day!

Tomorrow is
the first day of the
rest of our lives.

Terry Pratchett

IT'S THE SMALL THINGS

Even when everything seems bleak, there's always hope to be found if you look closely enough. Pay attention to those little things that seem insignificant: a new flower blooming outside your window, strangers smiling at each other or the simple pleasure of a slice of cake. Nourish yourself with these little seeds of hope and the feeling will soon grow. If you appreciate the small things, you'll be able to see that joy and beauty can be found in every day.

Beauty is everywhere
– you only have to
look to see it.

Bob Ross

YOU'RE IN CONTROL

Feelings of hopelessness and a lack of control frequently go hand-in-hand. Worldwide events and big changes can leave us believing that nothing we do could ever make a difference. While you may not achieve world peace or halt a global health crisis in your lifetime, there are always things about your life that you can control. Taking action in a small way, like contributing to your local community, can help you regain that sense of control and build resilience.

May your choices
reflect your hopes,
not your fears.

Nelson Mandela

I'm not afraid of **storms**, for I'm learning how to sail my **ship**.

Louisa May Alcott

IF WINTER COMES, CAN SPRING BE FAR BEHIND?

Percy Bysshe Shelley

GO EASY ON YOURSELF

Feeling hopeful is hard in difficult times, and it's okay to acknowledge that. When things go wrong it can feel like an impossible task to cling to optimism. You might be thinking, "How can everything possibly turn out okay?" But being hopeful isn't about believing that everything is going to be amazing all the time. Life is a mix of good and bad and everything in between, so give yourself permission to feel your feelings instead of fighting them. You don't have to be falsely chipper and upbeat about everything – that would be exhausting! Instead, go easy on yourself and remember that it's perfectly possible to have worries and anxieties, to feel low or sad, or to complain about things from time to time, while at the same time maintaining quiet hope that some good things are sure to come your way.

CREATE HOPE

Nourish your mind by embarking on a new artistic endeavour. Try painting, sewing, knitting, pottery or bookbinding – whatever you choose, seeing a project grow over time will fill you with a sense of accomplishment and give you something to look forward to. As well as levelling up your skills, making something with your own hands is incredibly fulfilling and can boost your enthusiasm for life. You could even make presents for your friends and family, and find joy in bringing joy to someone else.

However bad life may seem, there is always something you can do and succeed at. While there's life, there is hope.

Stephen Hawking

KEEP A HOPE JOURNAL

Keep a record of all the things that fill you with optimism that you can turn to when you're struggling to find reasons to be hopeful. First, get hold of a notebook or scrapbook; this will become your new hope journal. Any time you come across something that makes you hopeful – maybe it's a positive story in the news, a beautiful fallen leaf from an autumnal walk or something that someone said that made you smile – write or stick it into your journal. You could also include memorabilia, such as tickets from events or photos from happy times in your life. Ask your friends and family to send you postcards with uplifting, hopeful messages on them, and pop these into your journal too. Before long, you'll have a personalized book that's bursting with positivity and good vibes, and you'll be able to dip in whenever you need a pick-me-up!

Live life when
you have it. Life is
a splendid gift –
there is nothing
small about it.

Florence Nightingale

The **good** and bad
things are what form us
as **people**... change
makes us grow.

Kate Winslet

CHERISH YOUR RELATIONSHIPS

Feeling hopeless can be a lonely experience, making us reluctant to be around other people. But your friends and family want to spend time with you and it might be just the thing you need to feel a bit brighter. Whenever you can, arrange to meet up with loved-ones for lunch, a trip out or a movie night. Even if you're not feeling up to it to begin with, it probably won't be long before you're laughing and feeling brighter.

Life is tough;
and if you have
the ability to laugh
at it, you have the
ability to enjoy it.

Salma Hayek

GROW THROUGH WHAT YOU GO THROUGH

Unfortunately, bad things happen and these are often things you don't have much control over. But being hopeful isn't about avoiding bad experiences altogether, it's about learning to overcome them and learn from them. Maybe things didn't go your way. Maybe you didn't land that dream job, or you're going through a difficult break-up. Try to find something positive that can come from your negative experiences. Perhaps now you can muster up the courage to ask your boss for a pay rise or some additional training, or perhaps being single will give you the opportunity to learn more about yourself and your needs (or finally indulge in that food/music/TV show your ex-partner hated). Finding meaning in the bad things that happen to you isn't easy, but it will make a huge impact on your resilience and your outlook on life.

It is a rough road
that leads to the
heights of greatness.

Seneca the Younger

Essentials to **happiness** in this life are something to do, something to **love**, and something to hope for.

Hector Garcia

LOOK AFTER YOURSELF

When things seem hopeless it's easy not to bother looking after yourself. But keeping up a regular self-care routine is important for boosting self-esteem and confidence, and can, in turn, lead to an increase in positive thoughts. Set aside time for skincare and personal hygiene, mindfulness or meditation, exercise and hobbies. Make sure you're getting enough rest and relaxation. The routine will add purpose and structure to each day and will teach your mind that you deserve to be treated well.

Life is not easy for
any of us. But what
of that? We must have
perseverance and
above all confidence
in ourselves.

Marie Curie

BALANCE YOUR BUDGET

When you can't afford to do the things you love or you're worried about paying for essentials, you are robbed of hope for future plans. If you're not doing it already, set up and maintain a budget – the easiest way to do this is through a banking app, most of which have built-in tools for tracking your spending in different categories such as bills, groceries and eating out. Once you know exactly what you're spending, you can identify possible areas where you could save money. Many banking apps offer the option of putting spend limits on your different categories to make this easy to track. Some also have a tool for rounding up your transactions and putting the spare change into your savings, which you might find is a good way to save a little extra cash for a rainy day or a small treat. This way, even though you're still earning the same amount of money, you'll feel more hopeful about the future and more capable of making plans.

GO GREEN

Climate change is a huge issue that leaves many people feeling powerless, but taking positive action to live a greener life can help inspire a more hopeful mindset. So keep on top of your recycling, avoid food waste by using up leftovers, use soap and shampoo bars to cut down on plastic and mend old clothes instead of throwing them out. Look online for many more eco-friendly tips. Restore your hope and help the planet at the same time!

You are never
too small to make
a difference.

Greta Thunberg

LEARN TO FORGIVE

Forgiving people whenever they've wronged us or upset us is difficult, but forgiving people is a powerful tool for spreading love and hope, as well as building your own resilience, confidence and faith in humanity. Every situation is different – you have to ask yourself: does this person deserve, or have they earned, my forgiveness? Is it worth the energy of inviting them back into my life? Sometimes the answer will be no, but most of the time it will be yes!

We need never be
hopeless because
we can never be
irreparably broken.

John Green

Extraordinary things
are always **hiding**
in places people never
think to **look**.

Jodi Picoult

I rarely end up
where I was intending
to go, but often I
end up somewhere
I needed to be.

Douglas Adams

BE INSPIRED

When you're feeling trapped in your own hopeless or negative thoughts, listen to someone else's story for a little while. Find an uplifting biography to read or an inspirational TED talk to watch. Ask your friends or family to tell you about a meaningful story in their life, about a time when they were able to persevere through a problem or when things turned out for the better. You might be surprised by how many experiences your loved-ones have been through and survived that are similar to your own! It will do you the world of good to get out of your own head for a little while and immerse yourself in other people's stories of hope and endurance. Plus, these tales of overcoming adversity will give you plenty of positive ammunition when you find you need a boost of optimism in your life.

I KNOW THE SUN WILL RISE IN THE MORNING, THAT THERE IS A LIGHT AT THE END OF EVERY TUNNEL.

Michael Morpurgo

Optimism is the
faith that leads to
achievement. Nothing
can be done without
hope and confidence.

Helen Keller

NOT TODAY, NEGATIVE NANCY

Surrounding yourself with pessimistic people is a sure-fire way to feel hopeless about life. Think about the people you interact with at work, in your social life and on social media. Are there sources of negative energy that could be avoided? Muting or unfollowing people on social media, or spending a bit less time with downers and doom-and-gloomers, might make it easier to maintain a hopeful outlook on life.

It takes a lot of hard work to **remain** positive, but positivity **always** pays off.

RuPaul

BELIEVE IN GOOD THINGS

If you think today will be a bad day, then it's almost guaranteed to be. You'll only remember the things that go wrong, seemingly confirming that you were right all along. Next time you catch yourself thinking this, acknowledge the thought, then set it aside and focus on all the good things that are coming up that day, even if it's just dinner and a hot bath. If you believe that it will be a good day, then – guess what – it probably will!

I wake up every
morning believing
today is going to be
better than yesterday.

Will Smith

BE A PROACTIVE PROFESSIONAL

Feeling stuck in a dead-end job can be a huge cause of hopelessness. You might feel trapped in a career you're not enthusiastic about, or that there's no way of progressing, but there are always things you can do to take control of your professional development. Take advantage of any training and learning opportunities that arise; if you're feeling confident, you could ask your boss to be put on a certain project or be given the chance to develop one of your ideas. If all else fails, make a list of all the skills you've developed in your current position and use these when you're applying for new jobs. Taking control, even in a small way, might help you regain some enthusiasm for your working life.

THE WORLD BREAKS EVERYONE AND AFTERWARD MANY ARE STRONG AT THE BROKEN PLACES.

Ernest Hemingway

There's always
tomorrow and it
always gets better.

Ariana Grande

LIGHTEN UP

Are you getting enough natural light? Spending too much time in the gloom can leave you feeling, well, gloomy. Natural light has a host of health benefits including improving your sleep, sharpening your focus and lifting your mood. For many people, just being able to see the sun makes them feel more hopeful about their day. So try to get outside as much as possible, work beside a window and use light colours and plenty of mirrors in your home.

There is always light if
only we're brave enough
to see it, if only we're
brave enough to be it.

Amanda Gorman

NEVER GIVE UP

Everyone feels like giving up from time to time. When things are tough and you're faced with setback after setback, it's hard to find the energy to keep moving forward. But giving up is the surest way to guarantee you'll never reach your goals! Did you know that Stephen King's first novel, *Carrie,* was rejected by publishers 30 times? Or that Walt Disney was fired from a newspaper and told he "lacked imagination and had no good ideas"? Imagine if King had given up after rejection number 29, or if Disney had thrown away his dreams and ambitions. Luckily, they didn't – they never gave up hope that one day they would succeed. Each failure was a stepping stone edging them closer to their goals. Channel your inner Stephen King or Walt Disney to keep you motivated and hopeful during times when it feels like you'll never succeed. Just remember, you don't have to be an international bestseller or revolutionize the film and entertainment industries to be a success!

You can, you should, and if you're brave enough to start, you will.

Stephen King

No matter what happens, or how bad it seems today, life does go on, and it will be better tomorrow.

Maya Angelou

GIVE IT A GO

Think of that one hobby, craft or sport that you've always wanted to try. What's stopping you? Taking up a new hobby will get you feeling excited about life (or even just the weekend) again and will give you something to work toward. Having that sense of purpose and accomplishment as you progress in your new passion will bolster self-worth, confidence and, yes, optimism. If you attend classes, you might even make some new friends!

If you truly pour
your heart into what
you believe in...
amazing things can
and will happen.

Emma Watson

A FRIENDLY REMINDER

If you have little hope in your ability to succeed, remember times from your past when you achieved a goal or overcame adversity. If you're struggling to come up with anything, why not ask your friends or family if they can think of times when they were proud of you. They'll probably come up with loads of examples you never would have thought of! We are our own worst critics, so doing something like this might help remind you how capable you are.

Just believe in yourself.
Even if you don't,
pretend that you do and,
at some point, you will.

Venus Williams

Every **twist** and turn in **life** is an opportunity to **learn** something new about **yourself**.

Jameela Jamil

You are enough,
just as you are.

Meghan, Duchess of Sussex

YOU'RE HAVING A LAUGH

They say that laughter is the best medicine. And, whoever they are, they're right! Laughing releases feel-good endorphins which can decrease stress and worry and leave you feeling brighter and more joyful. Laughing with others can also strengthen your relationships with them. It's free and fast-acting, making it an excellent resource for countering negativity. So watch a funny film, relive some family in-jokes with relatives or attend a comedy night with some pals. There you go – you're having a laugh!

IF YOU SMILE, THINGS WILL WORK OUT.

Serena Williams

GOOD FOOD, GOOD MOOD

It may seem obvious, but it's important to eat well for your physical and mental health. Eating a healthy, balanced diet contributes to an improved mood and increased focus and energy, making you more positive and more capable of dealing with life's challenges. Make sure to eat plenty of fruit and vegetables, don't skip breakfast, and try to avoid too much alcohol, caffeine and too many sugary snacks. Give your body the fuel it needs to keep going through tough times!

Whatever you're
going through in
your life, don't
ever give up.

Mariah Carey

PUT DOWN ROOTS

Do you feel grounded in your community? Does your local area feel like a home, or just the place where you happen to live? It might not feel like your community has much to do with how hopeful you feel, but being involved with local initiatives and getting to know the people around you can have a huge impact on your sense of purpose and fulfilment. So why not get out and support your local businesses, sign up for that pottery class or charity run, attend or take part in the May Day parade, or make some friends at the farmers' market? Not only will you be contributing to local life and investing in the future of your community, but you'll have plenty of events to look forward to and new friends to keep you motivated. You might even enjoy yourself! When you get involved, hoping for the future stops being a vague thought and becomes a concrete action.

WALK IT OFF

If you keep getting distracted by negative thoughts, try going for a walk. The change of scenery will refresh your mind and help you break away from the cycle of hopeless thoughts, and the exercise and fresh air will give you an energy and mood boost. Plus, a walk will give you time to reflect on and challenge the thoughts that are dragging you down. It's amazing how much brighter things feel when you're out in the open air!

If you're walking
down the right path
and you're willing to
keep walking, eventually
you'll make progress.

Barack Obama

THREE GOOD THINGS

As we go through each day, we're more likely to remember the things that went wrong, and forget about all the good things that happened. This skews our perception of how the day went, and, in turn, how we feel about the days coming up. So if you often find yourself at the end of the day believing nothing went right, sit down for five minutes and think of three good things that happened instead. Maybe your boss complimented you on your work, you got a new personal best on your run or you cooked a delicious new recipe for dinner. Write these down in a notebook and, if you do it every day, you'll soon have a record of lots of lovely things that have happened to you every single day of your life. Read your notebook back whenever you need to be reminded that good things happen every day, in whatever form they take!

There are so many **great** things in life; why dwell on **negativity**?

Zendaya

Just don't give up
trying to do what you
really want to do.

Ella Fitzgerald

DREAM VACATION

There's probably one holiday you've always wanted to go on, but for whatever reason, your situation has prevented you from going. Why not plan it anyway? Go crazy! What's stopping you dreaming about the most expensive item from the fanciest restaurant, or researching the swankiest room at the chicest hotel? Planning for this ridiculous holiday might just be the escapism you need. Besides, you never know when your dream trip might become a possibility, and your plans will come in handy.

WHATEVER THE MIND CAN CONCEIVE AND BELIEVE, IT CAN ACHIEVE.

Napoleon Hill

WITH THE NEW DAY COMES NEW STRENGTH AND NEW THOUGHTS.

Eleanor Roosevelt

A journey of a
thousand miles begins
with a single step.

Lao Tzu

DREAM BIG, START SMALL

Big goals are intimidating! Whether you want to land that ideal job, buy your dream home or finally achieve the ultimate bucket-list experience, an ambitious target can seem like such a huge task that many people are put off from even taking the first step. Our dreams often stay dreams because they are so far removed from our current realities that we lose hope and give up. Long-term goals are a positive thing to have – they give you focus and drive. But it's important to break them down into small steps so that they don't seem so overwhelming and unachievable. Take your big goals and keep breaking them down into smaller steps, then break those smaller steps into even smaller steps. What's one thing you can do today to edge a little closer to your aim? Maybe you can spend an hour researching the industry you want to work in, or put aside a little money for your dream holiday. There is always something you can do, so there is always a reason to keep hoping!

My **mindset** is
to... take everything
one **day** at a time,
one step at a **time**.

Simone Biles

I am prepared
for the worst, but
hope for the best.

Benjamin Disraeli

SHARING IS CARING

Never underestimate the power of sharing your troubles with loved-ones. Maintaining a strong support network is one of the best ways to nurture ongoing hope. Meet up with a trusted friend or relative and share your fears and worries. You can chat (or moan) about the state of the world, or talk through your own personal concerns. Ask for their advice if you like, but even without it you'll be surprised how uplifted you feel simply by letting it all out.

Tough times never last,
but tough people do!

Robert H. Schuller

FEEL THE BEAT

Music is excellent medicine. We all have those songs that have the power to lift even our most miserable moods. Create a "hopeful playlist" of uplifting, inspiring or motivational tracks that give you the energy to keep going. Better still, include songs that have meaning to you or remind you of special people or happy events in your life. You can then listen to your playlist whenever you need a quick burst of positive and hopeful vibes.

Every **day** brings a chance for you to draw in a breath, **kick** off **your** shoes, and dance.

Oprah Winfrey

JUST RELAX

Going through difficult times takes a toll on our bodies, so it's important to relax and go easy on ourselves. Your body is amazing and it's got you through everything life has thrown at you so far, so make sure to give it plenty of love and care. Develop (and stick to) a good sleep routine: go to bed and get up at the same time each day, wind down with something relaxing, like a good book, and avoid screens and phones for two hours before bed. Try setting aside five minutes each day for some deep breathing exercises to keep you feeling relaxed and centred.

Soothe tired muscles and skin with a weekly bath or face mask. Relaxed bodies are so much better able to deal with the challenges of life, so try introducing some of these practices into your routine and see what a difference it makes to your well-being and hopefulness!

NOTHING IS WORTH MORE THAN LAUGHTER. IT IS STRENGTH TO LAUGH AND TO ABANDON ONESELF, TO BE LIGHT.

Frida Kahlo

If you're feeling low, don't despair. The sun has a sinking spell every night, but it comes back up every morning.

Dolly Parton

INVEST IN NATURE

Planting a tree is an excellent way of giving back to our beautiful planet. It can also fill you with hope for the future through the power of growth. If you have a garden, great! Research species suited to your climate and space allowance and you can plant your tree right away. If not, see if there are any tree-planting initiatives or community projects nearby. As you watch your tree grow, nourish yourself on the hope of the new life sustained within its branches.

Adopt the pace of
nature. Her secret
is patience.

Ralph Waldo Emerson

HOPE HEROES

Find a "hope hero" – a person who inspires you that you can look toward when you're feeling downhearted. It could be someone famous or someone known to you, as long as their story resonates with you and fills you with hope. Here are three examples of hope heroes to get you started: Nelson Mandela, Helen Keller and Cinderella. Nelson Mandela endured 27 years in prison for trying to overthrow South Africa's apartheid system and went on to become his country's president. Helen Keller lost her sight and hearing as a baby, but that didn't stop her becoming a successful author and advocate for disability rights, women's suffrage and world peace. Cinderella might be fictional, but she never stopped believing and hoping for a better future, even though her life was difficult and her relatives cruel. Once you've chosen your hope hero (or maybe you picked a few!), they can act as a reminder to never lose hope, even when things feel like they'll never get better.

Part of being optimistic is keeping one's head pointed toward the sun, one's feet moving forward.

Nelson Mandela

EVERYTHING THAT IS DONE IN THE WORLD IS DONE BY HOPE.

Martin Luther

LOVE OUT LOUD

Love and hope go hand-in-hand. When you spread love and offer it up to others, it grows within you and feeds your hope for the future. So express your love! Hug all your friends, give your significant other a kiss and ring up your family to tell them how much you love them. The more you show love, the more you will feel it in return, and the more it will boost your *joie de vivre*.

EVEN THE DARKEST NIGHT WILL END AND THE SUN WILL RISE.

Victor Hugo

If you're interested in finding out more about our books, find us on Facebook at Summersdale Publishers, on Twitter at @Summersdale and on Instagram at @SummersdalePublishers.

www.summersdale.com

All the **happiness**
there is in this world
arises from wishing
others to be **happy**.

Shantideva

EVERYTHING PASSES

In times of struggle and hardship, it might seem like things will go on this way forever and will never get better. But remember this: everything passes. If you're struggling to see the light at the end of the tunnel, think about times of difficulty throughout history, in your own life or in the lives of your loved-ones. Periods of war, disaster or financial depression across the world have passed. Sure, the road to recovery is long and has many twists and turns, but change and healing do happen, even if progress is slow. Maybe you have suffered an illness, job loss or bereavement in the past. At the time it might have felt like you'd always feel that pain, but gradually things got brighter and you were able to start enjoying life again. So, it stands to reason that what you are going through right now will also pass. Just being able to acknowledge that things aren't always going to be this way will help you become more hopeful. Remember: there are always brighter days ahead.

When you reach
the end of your
rope, tie a knot in
it and hang on.

Anonymous